GOD,
WHEN WILL I GET
MARRIED?

God, When Will I Get Married?
Copyright © 2012 Laura Reyes

All rights reserved.

All Scripture quotations are taken from the New King James version of the Holy Bible.

ISBN: 978-0-615-77175-5

EDITORS: Merlene Purkiss; Annette Johnson, Allwrite Publishing

PHOTO: Xavier George

DEDICATION

This book is dedicated to my loving husband, Jesus Reyes, who is my best friend and soul mate. You are, no doubt, the greatest treasure God has ever given me, and I thank Him for uniting us. Thank you for always loving me, believing in me and for showing me what a true man of God is like.

CONTENTS

Introduction………………………………...…… i

1 – Finding Your Identity …………………...…….. 5

2 – What's Your Purpose? ………………….…. 18

3 – Moving On …………………………….…….... 27

4 – Dress to Impress ……………………….. 38

5 – Get a Life ……………………………….…. 46

6 – Setting Boundaries …………………….…..... 59

7 – Nine Secrets to Finding the One ……….…... 68

8 – God's Timing ……………………………... 84

9 – Do's and Don'ts ……………………….…... 94

10 – How Do I Know If It's God's Will? ….....…100

About the Author ……………………….…. 112

INTRODUCTION

But those who wait on the LORD
Shall renew *their* strength;
They shall mount up with wings like eagles,
They shall run and not be weary,
They shall walk and not faint.

(Isaiah 40:31, NKJV)

We all have a desire to love and be loved; we all want to be with that special someone who God has for us, and sometimes as time goes by, we wonder, "When will it finally be my turn?" We want to love, we want to be accepted, and we yearn to find that special person. At times, when we see time passing and we are getting older, we wonder if God forgot about us or if something is wrong with us. In our state of desperation, we sometimes try to run ahead of God, and in doing so, we seem to attract the wrong mates.

As someone who had been heartbroken, hurt and waited on God for my soul mate, I remember reading many books on what I should expect and how to find the perfect person. Some even suggested that if I did my hair a certain way or acted a certain way, then, maybe, someone would notice me. Throughout that whole season of my life, I realized that none of those suggestions were able to help me because after I read all the books, went to all of the seminars, and heard all of the sermons about relationships, it all came down to me and God. I realized that I didn't have to act like everyone else to attract the right person. All it took was for me to realize that I should put my trust and confidence in God and that He had it all under control.

Sometimes I would get inpatient and wonder if God didn't hear me or maybe the desire in my heart wasn't what He wanted for me. I would see others getting married and having their desires and prayers answered, and I was still waiting. I really thought God maybe didn't want me to be married. However, I desired it, and I longed for the day I would get married. People used to tell me, "Don't worry. Your time will come. Just wait on God, and when you least expect it, it will happen."

For me that advice did not make me feel any better. In fact, it would actually make me feel worse. Sometimes I would say to myself, "Yeah, that's easy to say when you're married!" Nevertheless, I waited and God answered my prayer. In the middle of me falling in love with God all over again, He gave me confidence and identity, and when I least expected it, He sent me my soul mate, a reflection of His love in the physical.

With this book, I want to help you look into yourself and put away past hurts and issues that could be hindering your relationships. I also want you to know the importance of giving yourself value, setting boundaries, and knowing that it's okay to have standards and expectations. I want to talk about taking care of yourself and not being afraid to take that first step of faith or being afraid of rejection. Remember, God is a God of impossibility! Learn to wait *in* God and not *for* God. While you wait *in* Him, He will take care of putting all the pieces together in your life that will lead to that special someone He has for you. When he or she comes, you will realize that God's plans are way better than the plans or choices we could have for ourselves. I will also share some stories of how God took me from ashes to beauty and how he healed me, restored me, and sent me my perfect match, the one that He created just for me. No matter how much I begged God, He knew the perfect timing and the person, and now when I look back, I am thankful that I waited for such a moment like this.

Chapter 1
Finding your Identity

Having one's identity intact increases the chance of having a wholesome, healthy relationship. One of the reasons, if not the reason, people allow themselves to get into bad relationships is because of a lack of identity. Lack of self-identity leads to making poor decisions because it is tied to low self-esteem and self-worth.

Someone who doesn't know who they are will always be seeking the approval of other people; they will do anything to please a person – even if it means hurting themselves. When you get into a relationship with no self-identity, you will always be expecting the other person to fill a void that only God is able to fill. I have decided to start the book with this chapter because our identity is at the root of the relationships we get into, the choices we make, and the reasons we sometimes can't seem to attract the right person. What you tolerate and what you allow says a lot about where your self-esteem is, as well as your identity in God.

Have you ever seen a person, perhaps you, who have gone out of his or her way to get the attention of another person? Sometimes you may even do things that you know the other person likes in order to get their attention. Before I met my husband, I had a crush on this guy I will call Ernie. I was new to the church that I was attending, and I really wanted to attract his attention. Ernie was part of the usher's ministry, so I decided to join the ministry too. The first week I served was a complete disaster. After some quick training on how to coordinate the offering buckets, I made a huge mess and got myself and everyone else off track. I knew that wasn't what I liked, but I wanted to do it anyway because that's what Ernie was doing, and I wanted him to know that I liked what he liked. I decided to stick it out another week, but I realized the issue wasn't just the offering buckets. I was given orders from the leader to take the crowd in a certain direction. Being new to the church, I wasn't completely sure where everything was. Thus, I sent the whole crowd to the opposite side of the church. It was truly a mess! I was terrible at that position, but I wanted to serve the Lord while getting Ernie's attention. After two weeks, I knew, for sure, that ushering was not God's calling for my life. My lack of self-identity in who I was and in what God called me to be, led me to make decisions based on what everyone else wanted or *thought* would benefit me or on what everyone else was doing. A month later, I quit the usher ministry, and I promised myself I would never change my identity to impress someone.

We all want to attract that one person we like, but if you attract someone based on false premise, you will live a lie that could be almost impossible to resolve. You want to attract someone who likes what you like and sees things the way you see them. Don't ever change who you are for someone else, for on your life's journey, the person God has for you will meet you halfway on that road, and together, you will continue walking to accomplish one purpose and one God-given assignment. You will need each other. What you have and what you offer is exactly what the other person needs and vice versa.

When you know who you are, you will behave confidently in your life's work and in God's calling. You don't have to join a particular ministry of the church because all the cool people are joining it. Instead, invest in and perfect what you love or are passionate about. People are attracted to confidence and passion. Your passion for what you are called

> Don't attract the wrong attention.

to do may be clearly evident, but it takes people who have established their own self-identity to appreciate and respect this. Having confidence will prevent another person from causing you to waver on those things that you love.

You don't want to attract the wrong attention, so be true to yourself at all times. You want someone to love you for you, not for what they think you should be. Remember, the way you start a relationship will be the same way you will have to maintain it. So if you pretend to love riding horses from the beginning, but deep inside you know it gives you the creeps, the other person will expect for that not to change. You can only "pretend" for so long before what you really feel emerges. So, be

confident in who you are and in your feelings and
desires from the beginning.

Hurt People

When people have been hurt, maybe from a past
relationship, they have emotional wounds that don't
always allow them to think soberly. Some of the worst
decisions you can make in your life is when you are in a
state of emotional hurt and pain. Remember, those who
are hurt will eventually
hurt others as well, not
because they want to but
because their own
bitterness and pain would

> *Never make a
> commitment to
> someone who has to
> think twice about you.*

lead the person to do things that they normally wouldn't.
If the other person in the relationship is in the same
emotional state as you, then this is just a plan for
disaster.

Never get into a relationship while you are hurt
or if you see that the other person lacks identity in God
as well. Hurt people usually have empty spaces in their
heart that need to be filled. They might look for others to

fill that void, but only God is able to fill it. Furthermore, when we expect others to do God's job, we end up worse than how we started. The good news is, however, that God says in his word that in our weakness, He is made strong, and in our weakness He will be glorified (2 Cor. 12:9-11).

Second-Guessing

Never make a commitment to someone who has to think twice about you. Sometimes when we want to be loved and be with someone so much we are willing to tolerate anything. When you find the right one, you will feel a sense of peace and assurance that only God can give. In other words, you don't have to question if the answer is yes or no. God's will is clear, so you don't have to think about your decision or try to convince yourself as to why you should probably be with that person.

If you met someone who is "unsure" or has to think twice about you, then you will know it's time for you to move on. Be firmly rooted in your identity to know what you deserve. If you know that you are a true child of God, then you deserve to be with someone who loves you and is so sure that you are the right one that he or she is willing to scream it to the world!

I liked Ernie for two years, and for two years, he wasn't sure about what he wanted or what the right thing was to do. One day he wanted to spend the rest of his life with me, and another day he just wasn't sure. He would call me one day and want to spend time with me, and after that, he would disappear for weeks. I was confused. I wanted someone to feel the same way I did.

I stayed in that situation for so long because I lacked self-identity and self-worth. I made decisions based on the person I wanted to attract or felt I needed, rather than on whom I was or what I actually needed. The truth is that I didn't know better at the time. I spent my time trying to impress him and have him

> *Love who you are and love what God is going to be doing.*

like me. I joined the usher's ministry, I tried to pray like him, and I even sacrificed my priorities to be with him. Meanwhile, he had no commitment to me. It took me two years to decide that enough is enough and that it was time for me to leave. If I would have known who I was or if I would have known my true worth and value, I would have walked away after hearing the first "I don't know."

Again, lack of self-identity leads to flawed decisions. It leads you to tolerate negative things and focus on the wrong things. Make the choice today to live a life full of identity and of self-value. Know you are worth it and deserve to be loved.

Adding to the Relationship

When you get into a relationship with the person God has for you, one of your responsibilities is for you to add to the relationship. When you have a lack of identity, you will constantly be pulling things from the other person who they were not called to do.

What would you bring to the table in a relationship? If you don't know, examine your life and take some time to ask the Holy Spirit to reveal to you those areas that need healing, stability or just a basic reminder of who God is in you. Bring emotional stability, bring confidence in who you are and in the decisions you make. Don't be double-minded or insecure. No matter what the other person does, it will never be enough for insecure people because nothing will fill that emptiness in their heart.

Realize that you must bring something to the table and not rely on another person to fill a void or define you. Marriage is ministry and will become your first ministry. Are you ready to take care of it and help it grow?

Loving Who You Are

How can you love someone if you don't even love yourself? It's impossible to give what you don't have inside. I'm not talking about being conceited or thinking that you are all that, but I'm talking about loving who you are and loving what God is going to do in your life. One of the main signs of people who lack self-identity or have low self-esteem is to show no love or value for themselves. When you love yourself, you don't allow people to just do or say anything to you because you're able to discern God's will and know when things need to be put to a stop. Every day, aim to be a better, happier you. Love who you are, and love what God is going to be doing so you don't fall into the trap of needing someone to come into your life to give you that love or value because you will already have it. This way, you are able to give love and receive love.

Competition

I believe this has occurred with every single one of us. We have looked at another person and wondered, "Why is that person married and I am not?" I have certainly done this before. We fall into the trap of comparing ourselves with others, and then we become discouraged when we don't have what they have. Everyone's timing and purpose is different. Thus, when we compare ourselves to others, we take on unhealthy competition that leads to making emotional or incorrect decisions.

Because my younger brother got married doesn't mean it's my time and that I have to marry the first or next person I meet. Make sure that when you are getting into a relationship with someone, your motives and your intentions are correct. Make sure you are with someone because you love that person and you see a future with that person, not because your best friend or sibling is married. Competition breeds jealousy and envy, all of which are displeasing to God.

When you know your identity, it doesn't matter if everyone around you is getting married;

> *Competition breeds jealousy and envy.*

remain firmly planted in God and know that He will fulfill the desire of your heart. You know that your time is coming. I know that this confidence may be easier said than done, especially when you have people in your life reminding you all the time. We all have that relative or friend who, at every wedding or reunion, will always ask why you are still single. Or, they will say, "Don't worry, sweetheart, you are next!" I know nothing can be as annoying, especially when it comes from someone who is already married. But it takes true character and enduring self-identity to have those things said to you and it not change your heart or motives.

Being You

It's normal for all of us to have role models and people we respect and admire, but it's not okay when you change your personality or who you are so you can be like them. You will never be happy trying to be someone else because that's not who you were meant to be. Be you, an original, unique person. Let there be no one else like you!

When I would see someone who prayed, spoke or behaved a certain way that I liked or admired, I tried to be like that person, only to later discover that I was no good at it. Similarly, if your friend gets a new haircut, don't run out to get the same one. Just because it looks good on him or her doesn't mean it will look good on you. Be yourself, having your own personality, style and look. When you try to be like anyone else, you disappoint God because you are telling Him that who He created is not good enough.

Let there be no one else like you.

If you have a strange laugh, then so what? It makes you unique. Maybe your hair is wild or you are shy. It doesn't make you any less of a person; it just makes you who you are. Know who you are and be proud of it.

In addition, don't change your personality because it's what you know someone else would want. Remember, how you first attracted them is how you will need to keep them. So, make sure who they fell in love with is the person you really are, not the one they think you are. Do you like art or you like to read? Don't hide those things because someone else doesn't like them. It's impossible to please the whole world, so don't be afraid to express your talents, passions and love. Remember, that "you are fearfully and wonderfully made by God" (Psalm 139:13-14).

Chapter 2
What's your Purpose?

God has called each and every one of us to a specific assignment and purpose. However, there are times when our calling requires other people in order for them to come to pass. When you marry someone, you're not only marrying the person, but you are marrying their dreams, visions and purpose. The moment you say, "I do," you are also saying you will unite with their vision and, together, make it one. Therefore, before you get into a relationship with someone, make sure that both of you are headed to the same place or at least the same direction.

The wrong mate can lead you to abort your calling and never complete your God-given assignment. "How can two walk together unless they agree" (Amos 3:3)? So, if your dream is to be a doctor and you meet someone who wants to be a musician, it may likely cause a strain in the relationship when one of you is always traveling and the other is on call with patients. I'm not saying that it cannot work, but make sure that both of you are on the same page from the beginning. Make sure you know your potential mate's goals and dreams.

Are you a person who dreams big and your greatest desire, for example, is to feed poor children all over the world? In this case, make sure your potential mate is the type of person who also has ministry-oriented aspirations or is willing to support your ministry. Make sure he is someone who can support your dreams, appreciate them, and their passion complements yours. Are you ready to uplift the other person when she becomes discouraged about her vision? Are you willing to help them get back up when things seem like they are not going well? When you both desire or are willing to head to the same place, then you both will be able to encourage each other when one falls. Together, you will accomplish the calling that God has for the both of you.

When you marry someone, you're not only marrying the person, but you are marrying their dreams

When you marry the right person, you will have one purpose, one vision and one God-given assignment. You will need each other.

Discovering Their Goals

Do you know your calling and where you want to go in life? What are your passions? Those things that you are passionate about are connected to your calling. Take time to really see what you want to do and create a plan. A person with a plan doesn't just dream; but wants to make their dreams a reality. You might not know all the details of exactly what you need to do, but you have an idea and as you take action and take steps of faith, God will lead you to the exact place you need to be.

I've never met anyone like my husband

> *A person with a plan doesn't just dream, but wants to make his dreams a reality.*

who has had such a clear, confident knowledge of what God has called him to do. Before we even started talking, I already knew his passion and calling were in government. When we started courting, one of the first

20

topics of conversation was everything we wanted to do in God. We discussed our life-long dreams and goals. My husband's aspirations had to do with government, and my dream was to write books that would minister to people everywhere. I asked myself if the lifestyle of a future politician was something I wanted or could live with? Obviously, our goals were not the same, but that didn't mean we couldn't be together. Still, I had to ask myself if his political aspirations were something I would support. Did I even believe in his cause? Was I willing to go with him to the end of the world to make it happen? I made that decision before I even said, "I do."

I knew exactly what I was getting into from the start. I knew the journey was going to be interesting, but I was willing to go for the ride. Who says I can't write my books and reach hundreds of people while I'm sitting next to my husband at a meeting in Congress? He needs me to help his calling come to pass, and I need him to make my calling come to pass. We need each other. I'm not trying to say that if you are a teacher, the only person you are supposed to marry is someone who works in education as well. You simply need to find the person who somehow complements your dreams so that the both of you are willing to aim for it together.

Go to the Right Places

Keep an open eye to those around you. If you're not into coffee, don't spend time at Starbucks trying to meet someone. If you're not into music, a concert won't be your best choice. If you keep your priorities in order, always remembering where you are headed, and the calling God has for your life, when someone comes around, discerning who might not be for you will be easier. Our good friend Robert would always say, "You might not know who the one is, but if you're well-grounded, you can definitely know who the one is not." God has a funny way of always giving us signs. As you continue your walk with the Lord, serving Him and working hard toward those things you want to accomplish, the right person will meet you half way, and together, you will go on the rest of journey with one vision and one purpose.

Go to the right places. Do you ever wonder why you can't seem to find a suitable person? Where are you hanging out? If what you are doing is not working, then it's time for you to change your environment. Join an interesting ministry, serve in a different area, meet new people or work at an event you like. Go to the type of places you love, and be with the type of people you love because you will have a greater chance of meeting someone with whom you are compatible.

While you are Sleeping

Did you know that God knows you want to be with someone? It's difficult when you are single and much time has passed, and you are still waiting on God, believing that He is working on your behalf and hasn't forgotten about you. The Bible says that it is not good for the man to be alone, so God made a suitable helper as his companion (Gen. 2:18).

Did you know that God knows you need to be with someone?

Genesis 2:25 says: "But for Adam, no suitable helper was found. So, the Lord God caused the man to fall into a deep sleep; and while he was sleeping, he took one of the man's ribs and closed up the place with flesh. Then the Lord God made a woman from the rib he had taken out of the man, and he brought her to the man." What happens when you sleep? When you sleep, your cells replenish themselves, so your body is being rejuvenated. Your body is gaining strength and energy for when you wake up, ready to take on what the day has ahead. Adam needed a helper, someone who would be there for him and help him, and together, they would accomplish what God had assigned. Adam's sleeping represented his waiting period. He realized he didn't want to be alone and that he couldn't do things efficiently on his own. Adam needed someone to be by his side. God placed that desire within Adam, and since it was placed there by God, only He could make it come to pass.

Adam was looking, but nothing around him completely fulfilled him. He was looking in his own strength to ultimately realize "no suitable helper was found" (Gen. 2:20). God put Adam in a deep sleep so that Adam could rest in God. Meanwhile, God could work on Adam's behalf to create that suitable partner just for him.

Maybe you have been looking and asking God when He is going to bring you a partner, the one you need. You might even realize that no one around you is a suitable helper, not because these individuals are not God's children but because they weren't meant for you. It's easy to become desperate and frustrated because you feel like God is never going to answer that prayer. You have been waiting and you don't know what God is doing or how He is going to do it, but one thing you can be sure of is that while you sleep (wait), you are being prepared and becoming stronger. God is working on your behalf to bring you that suitable helper who will not be perfect, but will be perfect for you.

Are you in that deep sleep in which you have no idea what is going on around you but that desire is inside your heart? While you are sleeping, God is working to bring you that special someone, and in the meantime, you are getting ready for the moment you wake up. You might not see anything happen, feel anything happening or even smell anything happening, but that doesn't mean that God is not working on your behalf. It doesn't mean that God is not up to something or working to put together everything that He has planned for you.

Chapter 3
Moving On

In order to make room for God's blessings, we have to be willing to let go of things in the past that are hindering our progression. One of the biggest hurts is being in love with someone who doesn't love you back and forgiving someone who hurt you. How can we love someone if there are still leftovers from another person inside our heart? You need to be willing to leave that person at the cross, allow God to take care of the details, and remember that you are loved. You must let go and let God do what He has planned for you.

Unforgiveness

It's not fair for the person who God has chosen for you to have to deal with someone else from your past. If you haven't moved on, you will be expecting that person to do and act the way the person from your past did. You won't do it with bad intentions, but you will do it because pieces of the man or woman from your past still linger in your heart.

When my husband, Jesus, and I first began dating, I was still going through a lot of emotional healing from my past. Jesus would say something or do something that I didn't like, so I would snap in a major way. I was always on the defense because I had a fear of getting taken advantage of or mistreated. I thank God for putting patience and love inside Jesus' heart to deal with me at that time in my life. Even though I thought the past had been over and I had moved on, hurt and unforgiveness was still in my heart. It showed in my attitude and behavior. I became *Letting go doesn't mean giving up.* defensive with everyone around me, and even though I allowed someone to mistreat me before, I wasn't going to let it happen again. In fact, everyone in my life at that time suffered the consequences of me not completely moving on.

Letting go doesn't mean giving up. It doesn't mean you're a quitter. It just means that you have enough love for yourself to walk away when the time calls for it. Marriage is a unity of two people who are both in love with each other and want to share the rest of their lives with each other. Because of the level of commitment, sincerity, and consideration required for a healthy relationship, we must bring a whole, clean heart that has no residue.

True forgiveness sets you free

Unforgiveness and lingering hurt from a past relationship ties you emotionally to that person. You might be asking, "God, why I'm I not married?" Maybe the answer is because you are not completely single or divorced emotionally yet. Maybe you are still spiritually tied to someone else. You cannot enter a new season in your life if you have not closed and finished another season of your life. True forgiveness sets you free and sets the other person free as well. It breaks down any walls you have created in your heart and allows for God's will to enter your life.

Forgiving Yourself

So you have messed up in the past, and now you feel guilty and cannot forgive yourself. What if I told you that if you truly repent from your heart, God will forgive you and forget it? Guilt and condemnation are not from God, and he cannot bless you if you are still holding on to guilt from your past. Forgiving yourself is the most important step to freedom.

Failing to forgive yourself causes feelings of rejection and hurt. When someone takes the initiative

> *The presence of God is the only place where you can find healing.*

of wanting to start a conversation with you or take you out, you don't feel worthy or as if you deserve it. Because of that, you reject what God could possibly be doing in your life. You think because of what happened previously, you cannot be with anyone. If God forgave you, why can't you forgive yourself? Not forgiving yourself is telling God that his forgiveness is not good enough. Make the decision to start over new and let the past be in the past. Know that you are dearly loved by God and worthy of love from a mate, no matter who you are and what you've done. Realize that the best is yet to come in your life because He left all your sins at the cross.

Entering His Presence

In my hard times, I became obsessed with being in God's presence. It was the only place I could run, cry and scream if I had to, and it was the place I could tell God exactly how I felt. I spent many days and many hours there. I was in love with Jesus, my husband, but I didn't want him to have to suffer because of my own hurt and insecurity.

> He wants to give us the desires of our hearts.

The presence of God is the only place where you can find healing, where you will find answers to your prayers, and where you can be yourself with God. In His presence, I was restored, healed, and transformed. It's where you can be intimate with God and where you will feel His love and that peace that truly does surpass all understanding. Nothing is too small or too big for God. Do you like a man who doesn't like you back? Get into

His presence. You gave your all in a relationship but the other person decided to be with someone else, and now you can't seem to forgive? Get into His presence. There is no place like His presence.

When you become real with God and ask Him to reveal hidden truths, you will realize why sometimes our prayers are unanswered. God is our Father, and He wants to give us the desires of our hearts, but sometimes we are the ones preventing our own blessings. Below are a couple reasons for unanswered prayer:

- **No Relationship with God:** If you do not spend time in the presence of God, how can you expect to have a relationship with Him? If you have no communication with the person who you like, there is no way for you to have a relationship with him or her. Well, it works the same way with God. When you communicate with God and you are real with how you feel and what you are going through, God will make sure He reveals Himself to you. He will heal you and help you move on. He will also give you the peace you need to let you know that He has your back. "If you abide in me, and my words abide in you, you will ask what you desire, and it shall be done for you" (John 15:7).

- **Hidden Sin:** You may be able to hide your sin from other people, but you can never hide it from God. In Psalm 139:8, David says, "If I ascend into heaven, you are there; if I make my bed in hell, behold, you are there." So, everyone might not know that you are sneaking in that man or woman in your room every night, but God sees and knows all. So, when you question God about why are you not married and why He hasn't blessed you with someone special, take a good look at your life and see if there is any hidden sin or unholy behavior that is preventing you from getting a breakthrough. Psalm 66:18 says, "If I have cherished iniquity in my heart, the Lord will not hear me." Search your heart and ask God to give you a clean heart. Make the decision to get rid of the hidden sins that could be hindering God's blessings in your life.

- **Is it God's Will?** Are you praying for a mate and no matter how much you prayed, nothing seems to happen? God's will is perfect, and it brings peace and joy. Sometimes we like someone so much, and we think we have joy and peace, but it is really our flesh wanting to be with that person. Do you remember Ernie? When I liked him, I was convinced he was the one. I thought I had peace and joy. Although he disrespected me and all the signs and red flags were visible, I chose to ignore them. Then I would wonder why God wasn't answering my prayer.

God has an amazing way of always revealing His perfect will to us, but often times, the problem is that we are unwilling to listen and obey. I could have saved myself a lot of heartache and time if I had just paid attention to the red flags and listened to God's voice instead of convincing myself that Ernie was the one.

When I met my husband, everything aligned perfectly. Every desire of my heart was met. Everything I wanted and had asked God for, He answered. Even the slightest detail that I desired, God gave me. I wanted a man who was confident and knew what He wanted. I didn't want a man who was double-minded. I desired a man who is affectionate, funny, patient, and loves the little things I do, such as coffee. God gave me every desire of my heart. God is so good, for He even added a little on His own. My husband doesn't only love coffee, but he also knows how to make the best cappuccinos in town! Likewise, God's perfect will for your life will not lack any details. It brings joy, and it's the best thing you can ever experience.

- **Lack of Faith:** "Without faith, it is impossible to please God, because anyone who comes to Him must believe that He exists and that He rewards those who seek him" (Heb. 11:6). Do you pray and then doubt that

  A sense of expectancy activates your faith.

  God can make it happen? You cannot please God if you are not willing to believe that He will do what He promises. Faith moves mountains; faith makes the seemingly impossible possible in your life. You might think that the person God has for you will never come, but do you have faith to believe that it will? All it takes is a little faith for God to do incredible things in your life. You might be in a bad relationship that God wants for you to let go. However, it takes faith in God for you to let go and leave it all in His hands, knowing that He is looking out for your best interest and that He knows exactly what you need.

Restored Dreams

You long to be loved and to be in love, and because you were hurt, you feel as if you cannot open your heart to someone again. Let God restore your desire to be with someone. He has someone specially chosen for you who is waiting on you. You will know you have moved on and healed when your dreams and desires are restored.

Restored dreams give you a feeling of expectancy, and a sense of expectancy activates your faith. You know God is going to bless you, so you must believe and expect it. He knows what you want and desire, so He will do it if you trust Him. You don't have to worry, and you don't have to get discouraged because you know that God has your back. God says in his word, "For I know the plans I have for you," declares the LORD, "plans to prosper you and not to harm you, plans to give you hope and a future" (Jer. 29:11).

Chapter 4
Dress to Impress

As men and women of God, the way we look and present ourselves to others says a lot about who we are. Have you ever heard that the first impression is the most important? Well, it surely is!! Do you remember the last time you saw someone dressed indecently or completely ridiculous? When you saw that person, probably hundreds of things came to mind. Yes, we are not supposed to judge others, but one thing I have learned throughout my life is that you're biggest tool of evangelism is how you live your life! And this includes how you dress.

We are a walking testimony

Because we are a walking testimony, we have to make sure the way we dress reflects who we are called to be. No, you don't have to dress like a geek because you're a Christian. You can dress stylishly or even trendy and still show who you are in Christ. I'm sure we all know that one person who always walks into a room and looks as if he or she just has it all together, wearing nice clothes, well-groomed hair and nails, and fragrant cologne. On the inside, we may even wish to be like this person.

So, what do these people have that we don't? The difference is not money to buy nice clothes and accessories. The difference is confidence and self-respect. I want you to know that it's okay to love who you are, take care of yourself, and invest in yourself.

Confidence

Confidence attracts other people. When you are confident, other people can see it. So, if you feel like a million bucks, with time, others will think you're worth a million bucks, too. It's not about how much you spent on your outfit, but it's how you present yourself that matters. Take time to examine yourself to determine what needs to change. Maybe your clothes need some ironing, or maybe your nails need to be trimmed. Whatever it is,

Confidence attracts other people.

39

take the time to invest in you and you will see that it will make all the difference.

Don't get me wrong, I'm not trying to say that looks are everything. However, we are men and women of God, and we are the representation of God here on earth. So, we have to look like it. Ask God if the way you are presenting yourself to the world pleases him. Some people may be fine as is, and others might need some tweaking. I know I did!

Self-Esteem

A couple years ago I was on a complete journey of "finding myself." I had gone through a lot in the past years, and I was in the process of picking up all the broken pieces, including how I saw myself. I completely let myself go. I went from a woman who always had her nails done to a woman who didn't even care if her hair was brushed. I share this because sometimes the issue is not about not knowing what to wear, but rather about your self-esteem. Sometimes we just feel ugly on the inside, and it discourages us in taking the time to clean up or dress nice. One day, I sat in front of a mirror and took a good look at myself, and I didn't like what I was seeing. I saw a woman who forgot about herself, who had lost herself somewhere in this life's journey. I knew it was time for a makeover, not only a physical makeover but an internal makeover as well. The Word of God says in Romans 12:1, "Do not conform any longer to the pattern of this world, but be transformed by the renewing of your mind. Then you will be able to test and approve what God's will is—his good, pleasing and perfect will." All it takes is a transformation of your thinking, a change of mentality! All it takes is for you to say, "God, I want to experience your perfect will for my life, transform me in every area that I need. I want to please you in every way. Even in the way I present myself to the world, even in the way I see and love myself, the person whom you created, even in the way I feel and look."

> It's time to make some changes

It's time to make some changes, not only on the outside but starting on the inside. Walk confidently, knowing who you are, knowing that you are beautiful or handsome, knowing that God fearfully made you, and knowing that the person who God has for you sees you the way God's see you – perfect and exactly what he or she always wanted.

Has someone told you that you were ugly, dumb or fat? I think we all have experienced someone like that in our lives, but the moment you let those who harm you and say negative things to you control who you are, you have given them power over your life. Make the decision to let those things go, and forgive those who have hurt you and have said things to you that have made you feel insecure. Remember who you are in Christ, not in your critic's mind. That helps you throw away all those comments that obviously are not of God and helps you get back on the right track.

Say to yourself, "God has fearfully and wonderfully made me, and if I have stretch marks, so what? If my hair is brown, but the person I have a crush on prefers people with blonde hair, so what?" Don't change who you are so the person who you want to attract can like you. Just be you! Be the best you that you can be, and make sure you shine so bright that no one could possibly miss your light.

Walking Testimony

Is God pleased with the way you dress? Are there some things in your closet that need to be thrown in the trash? Dress in a way that clearly speaks who you are. This is about walking around like a true child of God. When you're comfortable or even proud of your appearance, insecurities will slowly start to vanish. And when you walk secure in who you are, dressed like a true woman or man of God, there will be nothing stopping you!

Sadly, most of us humans are visual, men more so than women. The Word of God says in 1 Samuel 16:7 "Man looks at the outward appearance, but the LORD looks at the heart." Unfortunately, men look at the outside. Are your clothes too tight? Is your shirt so sheer that people can see through it? Do your jeans sag so much that people can see your underwear? Did you take the time to brush your hair? All those little details matter because sometimes the way you dress determines the attention you will attract.

A woman is supposed to be a man's suitable helper, not his downfall. Thus, she must help him avoid temptation and instead encourage him to be closer to God. A man who has seen it all and that all the boys "talk" about her body parts, is not the girl that he will want to take home to his mom, she will probably be the girl that he just wants to talk to his buddies about.

By nature, human beings are never really satisfied, always wanting more. Once we have reached level one, for instance, we want to see if we can reach level two and so forth. Similarly, dressing in a seductive manner will lead to temptation and a desire for more. A man who has gotten to level one will naturally want to see what's on level two. On the other hand, a woman who is dressed decently demonstrates that she is someone to be respected and someone who loves herself. Moreover, she loves God enough to consider the men around her.

Dress to impress and allow your clothing to say positive things about you. You can be mysterious or somewhat daring in your attire, but still be temperate enough to represent God correctly.

Chapter 5
Get a Life

So, the man or woman you have been waiting for has not come yet. Are you going to sit and be depressed, or are you going to enjoy every day of your single life until that perfect someone comes along. Being single is not a curse, and the moment you learn to enjoy it and work to be the best person you can be, will be when you attract a suitable mate. When you are looking and trying to impress, it's obvious. However, when you are busy having a life and enjoying it, that will be obvious as well, and that type of attitude brings confidence, and confidence is attractive. I'm sure everyone has heard a married person say or a person in a relationship say, "When you least expect it, that person will come." That saying is very cliché, but it's also very true. Yes, it's still rather annoying, especially when it comes from

> *When you are looking and trying to impress, it's obvious*

someone who is married. When you least expect to meet someone maybe when you're at your college football game having a blast with your friends, studying at Starbucks, serving at a church event or simply taking a walk. You just never know what God is doing behind the scenes and what surprises He has in store for you.

Having your own interests and enjoying your life shows that you are secure in what you do and that you are happy with your life. It says that if someone comes around and then decides that they don't want to be with you, your world won't fall apart or you won't be left without knowing what to do. No one can come around and mess with that because your plans and identity are well grounded.

Have a plan, get a life, and live it to the fullest.

We all are guilty of the saying, "When this happens, I will do this." Well, you don't have to wait to be married or in relationship to achieve your goals or experience special moments. Yes, it would be great to do all those things with someone by your side, but the time will come for that. In the meantime, while you are single and waiting on God for that special someone, make the decision to have a life, your own life, where you live to the fullest. Aim to achieve everything you have ever wanted. Getting a life is not only about doing a bunch of things, but it's about taking a deep search within yourself and seeing those areas that could be hindering you from being in a relationship. So, put yourself together, be bold, and make the decision to live your best life yet.

Have a plan, get a life, and live it to the fullest. Has your dream always been to go on missions to Africa? Then go and make your dreams a reality. Plan that mission trip or plan that vacation to Paris. Whatever it is that you've always wanted to do, do it. Don't wait until you have someone so that you can do it. When that person comes along, you will build new memories and have new stories to tell, but in the meantime, while you wait, enjoy the fact that you are able to get up and be spontaneous. Making decisions like moving to Spain for the summer or spending a year in New York City won't affect anyone but you.

Don't Isolate Yourself

Isolation can be one of the darkest areas and feeling a person can encounter. We were wired to have relationships with other people. Not just romantic relationships but friendships, associations, as well as family interactions with other people. The word of God says, "Two are better than one, because they have a good return for their labor: If either of them falls down, one can help the other up" (Ecclesiastes 4:9). One by themselves can do a lot of things, but two or more people joined together can move mountains.

> We are drawn by love, we need to feel loved, and we need to love.

Isolation is a type of defense mechanism that we use to protect ourselves from rejection and the possibility of being hurt again. However, isolation can cause depression and gives room for the devil to put things in our head. The devil's tool is speaking lies to you and trying to convince you to believe something that you are not. When you are in a state of isolation, you begin to think a lot, and if you start to believe all the devil's lies, you will become depressed. The devil knows there is power in kingdom relationships. There could be times when maybe we feel sad because we don't feel like we fit in with the crowd, or maybe you have become so discouraged waiting for that soul mate that you have decided to give up and stop trying. That discouragement and sense of

> *Take the time to smile.*

depression that you feel affect the relationships we have with other people.

You need a mentor or friend who God can use to lift you up and remind you that everything is going to be alright. We are drawn by love, we need to feel loved, and we need to love. Pray for your circle of friends. Pray for your leaders and your family so that you might build relationships that edify and encourage. Pray that God always gives you the opportunity to love others no matter what you are going through in your life. You might be sad because the person who you know God has for you has not come yet, but make the decision not to isolate yourself and allow the devil to tell you lies. Make the decision to love others while you wait on God.

Smile

When you smile, it makes people feel comfortable around you. A smile represents a welcoming message and lets people know it's okay to talk to you and approach you. People who smile

> *Run away from people who never commit to anything*

often are happy people, and happiness is contagious. People like to be around happy people. No one likes to be around a grouch. Someone who is always sad, upset or angry and never talks to anyone becomes a people repellent.

Take the time to smile, to make the decision to take a positive, happy attitude and approach toward life. Take a moment to look around you at all the blessings that God has for you. Maybe God hasn't answered that prayer of you getting married yet, but you make the decision to smile at life and know that at the right moment, that prayer will be answered. Meanwhile, you smile because you are blessed, fulfilled, and exactly where you need to be at that exact moment in your life. God's will and seasons are something to smile about.

Be Committed

Commitment to your church, community, or work responsibilities says a lot about your willingness to commit to a relationship. Run away from people who never commit to anything or finish what they start. Be committed through both your words and actions.

Make a commitment to trust God and not be led by your own feelings. Do you run from the church that you are attending because your mentor or leader said something that you didn't like? What happens when your future spouse says something that you don't like or does something that hurts your feelings? We cannot run from things the moment they are not going our way. But a decision to commit to what God has given you makes you a mature and teachable person who God will use to do great and mighty things.

A lack of commitment is linked to the spirit of fear. Some of the reasons most individuals fear to commit are:

1. **Fear of Rejection:** Some people are afraid that they will not be accepted for who they are. Thus, they make the decision to never commit to

anything so that they never have to run the risk of not being accepted. These people have low self-esteem, and they don't think that with the help of God, they can make a relationship work. They may isolate themselves even though deep inside they long to be with someone. They fear the rejection that they could possibly experience in a relationship, so that fear paralyzes them from pursuing their dreams and taking the risk of getting to know someone.

2. **Fear of Failure:** They are afraid that if they start a relationship with someone, it might not work out, so instead of starting something that will fail in the future, they prefer to not commit to anything at all. Maybe you come from a family that has experienced divorce before or from a family where you have seen infidelity, and you say that instead of that happening to you, you rather not commit to anything. Deep inside, though, you do long to be loved and to be in a relationship. You get depressed and isolate

yourself because the fear that you have inside is not allowing you to take that step of faith.

3. **Fear of losing freedom:** Maybe you're a very independent person. You have your life together, your finances in order, or you are getting your education. You go in and out of your house as you please, and it's hard for you accept that, yes, you want to be with someone, but you do not want to lose the freedom to do what you want. I'm not going to say that marriage will be the same way that it is when you are single, but a healthy relationship respects each person's needs.

Before you enter a relationship, are you willing to die to your flesh and your wants? Maybe you want to go to a football game, but your spouse is feeling sick. Would you be willing to sacrifice the game? Maybe you know exactly what you want to do with your paycheck, but your husband or wife thinks differently. Are you going to run the other way or rebel and do what you please with the money instead? You have to be willing to have enough communication, love and trust that together, you can make anything work. If you fear commitment because you fear that you will lose your "freedom," then you are not ready to start a relationship, for one of the main things that makes a Godly relationship so successful is your ability to be as selfless as possible and to love the way God loves.

4. **Fear of Responsibility:** I would say this is one of the biggest reasons in fear of commitment in men. Men carry a big role in the relationship. God calls men to love their wives, to provide for them and to take care of them. Marriage is a team effort of three: God, the man, and the woman. Women are to be submissive to their husbands and be accountable to their husbands. Meanwhile, men are to be accountable to God. Men, as head of their households, are responsible to seek God before making a decision and are responsible to seek God for the direction of their family. That responsibility and weight will scare

many people, especially if you are a man who is not in the best economic state or your relationship with God is not where you think it should be.

Don't wait until you become a millionaire to get married or to launch the next best thing, or to ask that girl out, but know that everything you do will be a team effort. Don't fear responsibility because when you do, you are saying that God is not able to provide and guide you. That doesn't mean that you will not do your part, but that means that when you work hard to get your life together and to seek God, then God will take care of the parts of your life that you are unable to do.

Anyone who has fear lacks faith in God. You are saying that God's love, power and promises are not enough, and that He cannot do great things in your life. Yes, you will encounter times when you are rejected and when things that you try will probably fail. Maybe you see a girl that you really like and when you try to talk to her, she shuts you down. Remember, rejection is God's protection, and if you take that revelation and make it yours, you will encounter anything in faith, knowing that God has your back. If something didn't work out as you planned or desired, it is not because something is wrong with you, but it's because that wasn't God's plan for you. Believe in God and that He has your best interest in mind. "The righteous may fall seven times but still get up" (Prov. 24:16), so don't worry about failure. Have faith in God.

Get Involved

Get involved in the things around you. Join that club or be a part of that outreach program that you have always been interested in joining. The best way to meet someone is in places of your own interest because you know that everyone there enjoys the same things as you. Are you into politics? Well, join student government or a political organization because everyone there will have similar interests, passions and dreams as yours. Get involved in your church and in ministries. Meet people from all different cultures and places because that will make you more well-rounded, someone sensitive to the needs of others. Be bold and brave, and get involved in what you love because you never know who has been waiting all along for you to take that step.

Chapter 6
Setting Boundaries

---

2 Peter 3:17 says, "You therefore, beloved, knowing this beforehand, take care that you are not carried away with the error of lawless people and lose your own stability."

There is no way that you can have a healthy relationship if you didn't establish boundaries. Just like you wouldn't allow a stranger to just come in and out of your house or to take your things, it is the same way you should be able guard your heart and your life so that people don't abuse them. Sometimes we don't understand why we feel bitter, hurt, or bothered by certain people, and the reason is because we have allowed them to take whatever they want from us without any limits. We have to learn to say no even at the expense of losing a friendship or someone being hurt. We should all be able to get to the point in our lives where we know how to say "no" or "yes" even when we feel like saying otherwise.

When we set boundaries, we are creating balance in our lives. We are telling God that we are putting Him first and taking care of what He has given us. We cannot be afraid to say no to our family members when they are constantly demanding things from us. To say no to that person we are in a relationship with who is asking for something that is not in line with God's Word, and to even be

> *When we set boundaries, we are creating balance in our lives.*

firm and stand up to that person who is disrespecting us at work. Don't fall into the devil's trap of making you feel guilty if you cannot please everyone. Always remember that guilt is not from God. God will never make you feel bad or guilty about something. The Holy Spirit gives you discernment to be able to know what is from Him and what is not from Him. Guilt, with time, will create burden, and when you feel burdened, you will eventually get burn out. Why? Because you're not doing things out of conviction or out of a desire to please God, but rather, you are doing it to please other people. Maybe you feel like God would be upset if you didn't do what is asked of you, but be led by the Spirit and never by what other people think.

Putting God First

Looking back at all the times that I asked God where in the world He was, I can now see that His hand was there all along. In fact, He has never felt more real to me. I spent hours in His presence, seeking Him and wanting to know more about Him. I wanted to know what He was all about, and for the first time, I fell in love with God. I couldn't wait to talk to God and to hear from Him each day. I knew God had something in store for me, and I wanted to live every second of my life to honor Him. The more I served, the more I saw His hand at work, and little did I know that the man who God had chosen for me was serving right next to me the whole time. I had known him for years. The more we served together, the more we talked and the more I started to think I was crazy because feelings were starting to grow. I really thought I had lost it. In my mind, I had no plans of starting a relationship because I felt I still had a lot of internal work to be done, but God had an amazing surprise for me. Every day that went by confirmed the fact that God wanted us to be together, so we began to court.

My husband was the complete opposite of me. He was confident and knew exactly what he wanted. He had a clear vision of where God wanted to take him, and if someone knew boundaries, it was him. I could say that this was one of the things that made me fall in love with him. God used the confidence that he had to bring security and stability in my life. Coming from a previous relationship where the guy would one day feel one way, and the next day he would feel completely different, I forgot how to trust. Still, God gave my husband a supernatural grace to deal with me and the wounds that were still halfway opened.

I still carried some bricks in my heart that I didn't know how to handle on my own. When we started courting, my self-esteem was still a work in progress. For a long time, I thought the way a man would show me that he admired me and liked me is by allowing him to cross boundaries that are not to be crossed before marriage. I didn't know how to say no to a man, whom in my eyes, I thought cared for me. When I started courting my husband, though, he quickly set boundaries in our relationship. When we would go out at night, he would always bring a chaperone with us. If there is one thing I want to be in this book is to be real, so let me tell you that I would be so angry every time I went out with my fiancé, and he would bring along a friend. I desired his undivided attention, and when he put the brakes on me, I felt so rejected. I remember opening up my heart to him and telling him how I felt, and he would constantly remind me that because he loves me and wanted God's blessings over our relationship, he didn't want to cross any lines. Furthermore, he said that he respected and admired me. I wasn't used to that, and for the first time being with a man who truly loved, respected and wanted to spend the rest of his life with me was something I still couldn't completely understand.

God started to work in my life and in my heart, and slowly, He started to heal me from the insecurity and mindset that in order for me to feel admired and loved, I had to allow men to cross boundaries that were not in line with God's word or will. Songs of Solomon 8:4, says, "Do not awaken love before its time." Why would it say something like that? Because God created all those beautiful things to be enjoyed during marriage.

Do not allow people to hold hands with you, kiss you or even act like they are your boyfriend or girlfriend if they are unwilling to make a commitment to you. If the person who you are talking to or who you are into doesn't know what he wants or doesn't know if you are

Set boundaries and standards from the beginning

or are not the person for him, then that is your sign to walk away. Yes, you will need to go through a season or time of confirmation and waiting on God, but make sure the both of you are always on the same accord.

Set boundaries and standards from the beginning. This means that if you meet someone who you like and you allow them in areas that only a committed relationship is allowed to go into (holding hands, long talks at night, kissing, etc.), you have

63

allowed this person to take parts of your heart that really belong to the person who is willing to commit to you and you alone. Also, this will only delay you meeting or recognizing the person God has handpicked for you and who actually deserves all those different areas of your heart.

Respect Yourself

When you set boundaries, you are saying that you are a person who needs to be respected. How can you expect someone to respect you if you cannot even respect yourself? Saying no to temptation and no to that person who wants to go further than they should with you is letting this person know that if he/she wants a relationship with you, then he/she will have to be serious. Why would you pay for a shirt that you know you can get for free? Similarly, why would that guy decide to start something serious with you if he knows that he can get the benefits for free and without having to make a commitment? Respect and love yourself enough to set proper boundaries in your life that lets everyone know that you are a child of God, and if they want to be with you, then things would have to be done the right way – God's way.

In order to set boundaries in your life and with other people, you have to:

1. **Be clear and secure**: Don't be the person who says, no, you cannot kiss me or do this and that, and allow them to cross boundaries once and then try to enforce it again at a later time. Be clear about your boundaries, and don't be double-minded. People who are double-minded are hard to be taken seriously and are the type of people who are usually taken advantage of.

2. **Be honest**: Good communication is the key to any relationship, whether it is a romantic relationship, friendship or family member. From the very beginning, it's very important that the both of you be honest about your feelings and expectations. It will be impossible to be in a relationship with someone who doesn't want to be on the same page as you. If you are with someone who doesn't believe in waiting for sex

before marriage, and you believe strongly in that, it will only be a short time before this becomes a problem. This incompatibility can either cause the other person to fall into sin or cause the relationship to fail.

Setting boundaries says a lot about who you are in God and about your relationship with Him. Women who allow men to disrespect them show that their self-esteem is low and that she doesn't have love for herself. Be secure in who you are. Say no when you have to and respect yourself enough to not allow anyone to cross any boundaries that are not supposed to be crossed.

Chapter 7
Nine Secrets to Finding the One

God deals with everyone differently and has different timing and plans for everyone's life. So, no, I cannot tell you that if you do this or that, the one God has for you will come in your life the next day. However, what I can tell you from my own experience and from fellowshipping with hundreds of singles is that most of the time our delay is our fault. God could have had the one sitting right there waiting for us, but because we refuse to do a little transforming of our mind and heart, we miss out.

God is always faithful, and He delights in giving us the desires of our heart. Have you done your part, however? I truly believe that we should do the possible, and let God take care of the impossible. I also believe that there are aspects of our lives in which we have no control. So, I compiled nine secrets to getting yourself

on the road to finding the one God has chosen and
reserved for you.

Secret #1: Be confident

First, be confident that your Heavenly Father
loves you unconditionally, and being with someone is
not for the purpose of filling a void in your heart that
only belongs to God. You
want to be with someone
because you are ready to spend
the rest of your life with that

*You are a walking
representation of
God*

special someone to share your dreams and passions so
that together, you can form a relationship that is
grounded and rooted in God. Essentially, being
confident is not being conceited; it's having a complete,
full understanding of who you are in God.

Second, you should not only seek to feed
yourself spiritually, but you should also ensure that your
outward appearance exudes confidence. This confidence
comes from enhancing the things that make you special
or unique while improving those details that you need to
in order to look and feel your best. Remember, you are a

walking representation of God, and the way you dress and look should demonstrate that. Because you're a Christian, it doesn't mean you have to dress like a geek, but it does mean that your clothes should not send the wrong message.

Secret #2: Surround yourself with like-minded people

My husband and I were in the same discipleship group together for three years, and even though we were just friends for a long time, God had put a holy veil over our eyes that was not removed until God's timing. We served together and did events together. We also taught groups and mentored together. We both had the same vision and love for God. We, in fact, had a passion for His people. We wanted to be used outside of the church walls, and God united us so that together, we could accomplish His assignment. We were focused on seeking God, and in the process, God united us.

Once you have a clear vision of your calling and purpose, you should surround yourself with those who you know have similar passions as you. For example, as a believer and a man or woman of God, you should not spend time at bars and hope to meet someone nice there. I'm not saying that everyone who goes to clubs and bars are bad people, but are their priorities the same as yours? It's important for you to surround yourself with people who are going to edify your life and add to it, not subtract from it or distract you from your purpose.

Who are you surrounding yourself with? Do they share your passion? 1 Corinthians 15:33 says, "Bad company ruins good morals." Take a look at your circle of friends. Are there some friends who are pulling you away from the things of God? Surround yourself with those who believe in your calling and purpose. Also, make sure you surround yourself with people you can be yourself with, not those you have to pretend that you are more of this or less of that.

Secret #3: Don't compare yourself to others

Just because your younger sister or brother is getting married doesn't mean you have missed your train. Although the people around you are tying the knot doesn't mean God has forsaken or forgotten about you.

That's a lie from the devil, and all it does is lead you to make emotional decisions that are not led by God. I believe the enemy loves to have you compare yourself to other people because it makes you think that God is not aware of your heart's desire.

You need to break away from people's expectations

You need to reach a point in your life when you can see people around you being blessed, and you are genuinely happy for them, knowing that your blessing and promise will come, too. Your life is your life, and God has already planned everything He will do with you. It doesn't matter what good things are going on in everyone else's life, your time will come. The more you believe that, the lighter and more enjoyable your life will be.

Of course, people don't always make that too easy. I remember friends and family members saying, "So Laura, when are you going to get married? You are not getting any younger." Sometimes they would be more straightforward, "I can't believe [so and so] is married, so when is it going to be your turn?" All those

71

questions and pressure from other people would lead me to get depressed and wonder when my turn was going to come, and that maybe God had forgotten about me.

You need to break away from people's expectations for your life. Comparison is not of God. He has made you unique and with a specific plan and assignment. If you live your life comparing yourself to others, you will live without joy and peace because you are always looking at what God is doing for other people and not grateful for what He has already done or is going to do for you. Make a decision today to not worry so much about what's going on in the lives of those around you, but

You cannot be afraid to take the time to get to know someone

rather, focus and know that the best is yet to come in your life.

Secret #4: Don't be afraid of rejection

So, you dated John, and he turned out to be the wrong person for you. Then you met Johnny, and you really thought he was the one. It turned out, however, that he does not have the same feelings for you. You feel down, and your confidence is shattered because you can't handle the rejection. What God is really doing is protecting you from being with the wrong person. Most of the time, rejection is God's protection.

A bird and a cat are both creations from God. He loves, provides and protects them both, but are they meet to be together? If you put a cat and a bird together, the cat will eat the bird. Why? They just weren't made to co-exist in the same environment. Sometimes we are the bird, and we want to be with a cat. God is so amazing that even if it hurts us a bit, He wouldn't allow that incompatible relationship to happen because if it did, it would be a disaster.

If you don't ask her out, you will never get that date

You cannot be afraid to take the time to get to know someone because you are afraid of being rejected. Always remember that God is your best friend, and He is on your side. If you meet someone and it doesn't work out, it was because it wasn't meant to be, and not because something is wrong with you. When you are secure in who you are in God, being rejected will probably hurt for a while, but soon you will be able to recover and be excited for what God is going to do. Just because that cute guy from the gym doesn't ask you out on a date, it doesn't mean your prince is never going to come.

Men, you are the initiator. If you don't ask her out on a date, you will never get that date you secretly want. I know it could be sort of scary, but if you don't take that step of faith, you will never know what could have come out of that encounter. Just one bold decision can change your life forever.

Go out and enjoy your life.

Secret #5: Know how to hear from God

If you are able to hear God's voice, He will always give you peace or either no peace about a certain person. Maybe you really like this woman, but something inside of you doesn't give you that complete peace that you know is supposed to come with the package. Are you mature enough to know when God is speaking to you, warning you or telling you to walk away? So much heartbreak could be prevented and so many amazing things would be happening in our lives if we were able to know when God is speaking or leading us in the right path.

God knows your end from the beginning. He knows exactly who you are going to marry, where you are going to live and when you will probably not obey Him. He knows it all; there is nothing we can hide from Him. He is the perfect guide or Shepherd, but we have to recognize this through faith and realize where He is leading us. Thus, when you know His voice and He tells you to walk away from a relationship, you will obey.

So, how do you get to a point in your relationship with God that you are able to hear His voice? Just like any relationship, it requires that you spend time together and communicate. How is your prayer life? How is your faith? Do you really believe God wants the best for you?

With knowledge of God's ways and full confidence in Him, we will make better decisions and have greater peace. When you know how to hear God's voice, you won't need Him to send you a hundred signs to confirm that the person you are interested in is the one. God will give you a peace that "surpasses all understanding" (Phil. 4:7), and everything will align perfectly in His will for your life.

Secret # 6: Step out of your comfort zone

You must not be afraid of doing something different and taking risks. If what you have been doing all along is obviously not working, then it's time to change some things. You must not be afraid to think outside the box and take some bold steps. What do I mean by this? For instance, do you usually stay home on the weekends? Well, then it's time for you to get up and expand your circle. Go to that concert; spend some time studying at Starbucks or at your campus library. Go to that event that all your friends are attending. Get out and enjoy your life.

Isolation brings depression, and when people are depressed, you can see it all over their faces. No one wants to be around someone who doesn't like talking to people or just wants to stay home all the time. I'm a homebody, and I enjoy spending time at home watching movies. However, I would not have met my husband if I did that every weekend. While it's okay to spend some nights at home alone, it's not okay to never go out and meet people. God wants you to enjoy relationships and friendships. Despite what some think, He wants us to have fun and fellowship.

Step out of your normal routine, and when you do, it will make your life more interesting. Do something out of the ordinary like changing your wardrobe or trying a new hairstyle. You can even make attitude changes, such as deciding to listen to people more often. Whatever change you decide to make, just step out of your comfort zone and be more engaging.

Secret # 7: Maintain a positive, upbeat attitude

I've always heard that a smile is someone's best accessory. No one likes to be around someone who is negative all the time. When you are happy and have a positive attitude, it makes people feel more comfortable around you. They know you are approachable and pleasant, which, in itself, is attractive. If you allow God to direct your life, you should be positive, looking forward to where your life is headed through Him. Your life may not be perfect and there may be a lot that God is still dealing with you about, but you should still be content. After suffering many trials and tribulations, Paul could have questioned God's love, provision and protection, but instead, Paul said, "For I have learned, in whatever state I am, to be content" (Phil. 4:11).

Try to see the good in everything, and encourage people when you see them falling into the trap of negativity. People will always remember that. Smile often, walk with confidence, and be forgiving. Those who constantly forgive are some of the happiest people because they are not bound to any hurt from the past. They are able to give it to God and keep moving forward, knowing that God is in control of their lives.

A simple smile can attract all kinds of positive things to you. Thus, always try to be upbeat and positive, demonstrating the best in you and bringing out the best in other people. You don't know whose life you can change in the process.

Secret #8: Learn how to wait

You know God has that person already there for you, so you can wait in Him knowing that He will come through. Do you know the difference between waiting *in* God and waiting *for* God? When you wait *for* God, you try to dissect everything while focusing on when He's going to answer that prayer. You get desperate, stressing and wondering how He is going to do it and how everything is going to come together because right now, it doesn't make sense to you. When you are waiting *in* God, you don't have to understand everything and you don't have to reason about everything because you know that God delights in giving you the desires of your heart (Psalm 37:4). You prepare for that time and invest in yourself, so when that person comes, you are ready. You enjoy your wait and walk with a heart of expectancy, knowing that any day now, God is going to surprise you!

Secret #9: Have realistic expectations

Many women want to marry Channing Tatum, and most men would want to marry Jennifer Lopez. However, if the person you are interested in didn't look like an attractive celebrity but he/she has everything else you like, you should not walk away in search of perfection. Finding someone with the

Don't create false expectations

"perfect" looks, personality or career is unrealistic. Not everyone will be called to marry the next pastor, NBA player or beauty queen. Nonetheless, you can work together with that person and aim for a certain vision to accomplish great things. Perhaps, your spouse had a persistent dream or strong passion when you first met, but with teamwork, you can help him/her to actually fulfill those goals. In other words, God may only reveal a person's potential in the beginning, which may seem too imperfect for some people, but we have to be steadfast and supportive in order to witness the full manifestation and significance of that person's gifts and calling.

Don't create false expectations that will just make your waiting period frustrating and maybe longer than necessary. Dare to believe in someone's dream and dare to make it part of your own. Because when you do, you can create something beautiful together. Don't expect the person to always be perfect, because everyone comes with imperfections and flaws. Don't leave after the first thing they do wrong. Remember, you yourself, are not perfect, either. Even though they are certain flaws that cannot be tolerated, make the decision to find the person whose imperfections you can live with and that you balance each other out. Your weakness should be their strength and their strength your weakness.

I become emotional quickly, and my husband is very emotionally grounded. So, when I'm throwing a crying fit about something, my husband reminds me that everything is going to be okay. We create a balance for each other. Where I'm weak, he is stronger and helps me find stability in that area. Where he is weak, that is where I come in to help and be his other half.

Do create expectations, realistic ones, though. Never settle for anything but God's best for your life, but don't exclude someone because they don't fulfill your unrealistically high physical or other expectations. You are a child of God just like they are, so know when it's okay to be flexible inflexible. Ask God for discernment and wisdom when you meet someone, and be ready for God's best in your life.

Chapter 8
God's Timing

Nothing is more amazing than experiencing God's perfect timing in your life. It doesn't matter what area of your life it is, whether it is in relationships, your career or in ministry. When that time comes, you will experience a peace that surpasses all understanding, as well as God's special grace and favor. You will also recognize God's perfect timing because everything will align with His promises. Furthermore, God's timing and will do not bring confusion, hurt or strife. You don't have to try to force God's timing because He has an incredible way of putting all the pieces together, even when you least expect it.

We can only experience God's perfect timing when we yield our will to His will and ways. No matter what the situation may look like or how we may feel, we must learn to trust God in faith, knowing that His timing is perfect. His timing will always work best for our lives, others' needs or His plans. In other words, it works perfectly for everyone.

God's Perfect Timing

One of my favorite love stories in the Bible is the story of Ruth and Boaz. It is an example of God's perfect timing. It has such an amazing way of showing us how a man and a woman of God should behave in their waiting period and in the moment when they enter their season of promise.

Ruth, a Moabite, was Naomi's daughter-in-law, and while living in Moab, Naomi's two sons died, one of them being Ruth's husband, Mahlon. Naomi, a Jew, then decided that she wanted to return to her homeland of Jerusalem, where she heard that aid was being given to the Jews during the famine (Ruth 1:1-5). Naomi insisted that her two daughters-in-law return to their mothers' homes and even remarry (8-9), but Ruth refused to leave Naomi. No matter how much Naomi insisted, Ruth wanted to follow her mother-in-law (Ruth 1:16).

He orchestrates everything in our lives

While the other daughter-in-law remained in Moab, Ruth decided to leave everything behind to support Naomi. Ruth said, "Your people shall be my people, and your God, my God. Where you die, I will die" (Ruth 1:16-17). Once they relocated to Bethlehem, Ruth wanted to go out to the field to glean grain (Ruth 2:2). The field belonged to Boaz, a wealthy relative of Naomi's husband.

One thing I know for sure about God is that there are no coincidences with God. He orchestrates everything in our lives. We might not understand why we have our current job or attend a certain church, but God has everything set up for a reason. Ruth thought she was merely going to go look for work, but God had something else in mind. She was walking and working on the land of her future husband.

Sometimes we wonder why things happen to us, so we question God, but are we willing to set aside our feelings and allow God to lead us to His perfect will? Disobedience and lack of faith can delay God's promises in our lives. If Ruth would have gone back with her sister-in-law, yes, God may have still given her a husband, but not *the* husband He had ordained for her. God rewarded Ruth's faithfulness and willingness to forsake her pagan roots in Moab.

Are you willing to wait when God doesn't immediately give you what you desire? Are you secure in knowing that God has not forgotten about you and is working in your favor? Are you willing to move when God tells you to move, even if it looks as if the circumstances are not what you may have wanted or planned for? We have to be faithful and flexible to God's leading, remembering that His ways are higher than our ways (Isaiah 55:9).

Ultimately, Boaz noticed Ruth, seeing something unique in her; he asked his servants who she was. He asked Ruth not to look for work anywhere else because he wanted her to continue working in his field (Ruth 2:9). Boaz told Ruth that he would provide for her. He also asked his servants to look out for her.

Ruth said to Boaz, "Why have I found such favor in your eyes that you notice me —a foreigner?" (10). Do we have to fit in with the crowd? No, because sometimes a person's unique look or ways is what may catch someone else's attention, as it did with Boaz. When you are in God's perfect timing and in front of the right person, it doesn't matter where you are from or what you have done. God will give you favor in the eyes of the one who will notice you, and you will be considered special and fascinating.

Boaz told Ruth to sit with him and the harvesters to have some bread (Ruth 2:14). He was so amazed by her that he even had Ruth sit at his table and eat with him. He didn't care who saw or what other people thought. When you're with the right person, he/she is going to want to tell the world about you, for there is nothing to hide. You know you're not in the will of God if the person who you are with doesn't want anyone to know about you. Remember, God withholds no good thing from us (Psalm 84:11). Similarly, He tells us to make sure our light is visible to the world, never hidden (Matt. 5:14-16; Mark 4:21).

Ruth ate all she wanted and had some left over. As she got up to clean, Boaz gave orders to his men, "Let her gather among the sheaves and don't reprimand her. Even pull out some stalks for her from the bundles and leave them for her to pick up, and don't rebuke her" (16). Boaz stood up for Ruth and protected her. Likewise, God expects men to protect and provide for their wives. Do you feel that you are ready to take on that role in your life? You don't have to be rich, only be committed to your household and God.

God also uses accountability as a way of protecting us. Boaz was accountable to those around him; they knew and saw what he was doing. Whatever Boaz gave to Ruth, she shared with her mother-in-law. When

God uses accountability as a way of protecting us

Naomi saw everything Ruth brought, she asked Ruth where she had gotten all that grain. Ruth explained that she had worked in Boaz's field. Ruth was accountable to Naomi. Proverbs 4:1 says, "Listen, my sons, to a father's instruction; pay attention and gain understanding." God wants us to be accountable and heed the advice of those who He has placed over us or deemed as a wise guide for us. When we are accountable to a mentor, parent, minister, or even friend, there's a special protection and covering over our lives. Women are accountable to their husbands and men are accountable to God.

Naomi tells Ruth to wash and anoint herself, and put on her best garment (Ruth 3:3). Remember chapter 4 on dressing appropriately? Naomi wanted Ruth to look her best and then go back to where Boaz was with confidence. Although the way you feel on the inside, reflects your outward appearance, looking your best will help you feel more confident. Women should not only take care of their appearance, but men as well. Simple adjustments such as having your clothes ironed or shaving could make a huge difference.

Ruth lay at Boaz's feet, and when he realized that she was there, he asked who she was. She replied:

"I am your servant, Ruth," she said. "Spread the corner of your garment over me, since you are a guardian-redeemer of our family." 9 "The LORD bless you, my daughter," he replied. "This kindness is greater than that which you showed earlier: You have not run after the younger men, whether rich or poor.10 And now, my daughter, don't be afraid. I will do for you all you

ask. All the people of my town know that you are a woman of noble character.[11] Although it is true that I am a guardian-redeemer of our family, there is another who is more closely related than I. [12] Stay here for the night, and in the morning if he wants to do his duty as your guardian-redeemer, good; let him redeem you. But if he is not willing, as surely as the LORD lives I will do it. Lie here until morning."[13]

If you noticed, verse 10 says that Boaz realized that Ruth was not interested in whether he was rich or poor. Boaz saw a pure heart in Ruth and had fallen in love with her. What are your motives in entering a relationship? Are you interested in someone because they are rich or because they have a heart that loves and follows God? Our motives and intentions say a lot about our heart. God rejoices when our hearts are right with Him and our motives are aligned to His will. In verses 12 -13, Boaz realized he wanted to marry Ruth and he wanted to make sure he did everything according to God's will.

God expects things to be done in his order and the right way. Ruth did her part. She was accountable and waited on God. When it's God's timing, He will make everything perfect. Everything will just align without you even trying. Even when you feel you have met the right person, but it's the wrong time, this doesn't mean the person is right for you. If you remain faithful and obedient to God, He will orchestrate the events of your life so that you can experience the blessings of His will and timing. Habakkuk 2:3 says, "For the vision *is* yet for an appointed time; But at the end it will speak, and it will not lie. Though it tarries, wait for it; because it will surely come. It will not tarry."

Yes, your life needs to be in order, but God's order

Waiting on Perfection

Many believers are waiting on perfection, not God. They want their lives to be perfect before they seriously date or commit to someone. Again, you don't have to be a millionaire or wealthy to ask a woman to marry you, but make sure you will be able to provide for her. Also, don't fall into the trap of believing that if you don't have all your debt paid off, your cooking skills are not good, or you haven't completed your doctorate degree, then you are not ready to get married.

Yes, your life needs to be in order, but God's order, which doesn't require perfection but, rather, obedience. Take an honest look at yourself and ask God to reveal to you what areas in your life need tweaking. I knew I needed to deal with certain areas of my heart, such as my self-esteem before I got married. I've seen many instances with people when God placed someone in their lives but they reject the person because of all the standards and restrictions they have created for themselves. This makes me sad because God gave them the desire of their heart right in front of their face, and they literally can't see God's blessing because they are too busy trying to be perfect first. God doesn't want you to be perfect; He wants you to have a heart after Him and for every area of your life to be a reflection and a testimony of Him!

Chapter 9
Do's and Don'ts

God wants us to live life and live it more abundantly (John 10:10). This biblical principle is not merely about money and material prosperity, but it's also about living a truly joyful, peaceful, enriching life. Thus, you are to be with someone who truly loves you, respects you and sees your value. Although many examples and discussions have been provided in this book to help you find this someone, we all need some do's and don'ts for a clear understanding of what actions are either beneficial or detrimental, especially in new situations. The ones that are compiled in this chapter are not "thus says the Lord," but they are things that I have seen people do right or wrong, as well as my own mishaps that have come back to smack me in the face. For instance, I included rules as a result of comparing myself to others and worrying way too much about something to which only God has complete control.

Other rules center on times I ignored obvious red flags, but because I wanted to be in love and in a relationship so badly, I was willing to overlook the flags and tolerate any type of behavior as long as the person was happy and wanted to be with me.

Use these do's and don'ts, which review principles discussed throughout the book, to help navigate your journey in discovering the one God has for you.

Do's

- Dress appropriately (*1 Timothy 2:9-10*)
- Take care of your hygiene.
- Maintain your integrity.
- Be friendly; no one likes a grumpy person (*Ephesians 4:32*).
- Seek God with all your heart (*Deuteronomy 4:29*).
- Have someone to whom you can be accountable.
- Be prepared to be a wife or a husband.
- Get in the habit of saving money.
- Get rid of debt and any baggage that could ruin the marriage.

- From the beginning, set boundaries that align with God's will and Word.
- Respect yourself.
- Be yourself.
- Remember that God has not forgotten about you.
- Know that God wants the best for you.
- Know who you are in God and know that you are worth His best *(Psalms 139:14).*
- Be someone who can be trusted, and always keep your word *(Psalms 119:160).*
- Be happy *(Proverbs 17:22).*
- Pray in advance for the person who God has already selected for you. Pray in general for that person's protection and guidance so that God keeps that person pure, and always having a heart after God.
- Declare blessings over your life.
- Guard your heart *(Proverbs 4:23).*
- Do know when you have to stay away from or end a relationship.

Don'ts

- Don't believe those persons who tell you that God told them you are the one for them. When you meet the right person, God will make your feelings mutual, and you will feel a sense of peace and belonging.

- Don't compare those you meet with someone from your past who has hurt you *(Mark 2:22)*.

- Don't get married just because you want to have sex. Too many people get married quickly and later realize that the one they married were not for them.

- Don't get married because everyone around is getting married; get married because you know that you have found the one God has chosen for you.

- Don't compare yourself to other people because God takes everyone through a different journey and timing for a reason.

- Don't belittle others in front of other people to make yourself look good.

- Don't change who you are to please the other person. Know who you are, and don't change just because it's what the other person prefers. For example, if your hair is blonde and the guy you have a crush on likes brunettes, then it's time to find someone else who can accept you the way you are.
- Don't be afraid of rejection; in fact, don't let it stop you from taking the risk of getting to know someone. Rejection, at times, is protection from God *(Prov. 3:5-6)*. Remember, nothing is wrong with you just because someone rejects you.
- Don't worry because it gets you nowhere *(Matthew 6:34)*.
- Don't ignore red flags. They are God's way of telling you something is not aligned with His will for you.

Use these pointers to aim at being a better you, someone who attracts, as well as recognizes, special people sent from God. They should also help you become an enjoyable, balanced person who reflects God, as well as the true you!

Chapter 10
How do I know it's God's Will?

One of the main reasons people get into bad relationships is because they didn't take the time to seek God to see if the person who they are with or that they like is the will of God for their lives. Just because two people are Christians and they have similar likes doesn't mean they were meant to be together. So, how exactly do we know if the person we are with is the will of God for our life? Also, how do we recognize those red flags that God uses to warn us that something is wrong?

Red flags are signs that God uses to let you know it's time to walk away from a relationship. When we pray and ask if a certain someone is or is not the will of God for our lives, God has an amazing way of always making sure He answers that question for us. He gives us all the red flags, as well as confirmations, we need. These signs, however, require us to have our spiritual eyes and ears open to be able to discern God's will. If you want to know if someone is or is not God's will for your life, you have to be willing to put your emotions aside and make the decision to listen to what God wants.

At times, we want to be in a relationship so badly that we will ignore whatever sign God sends us. As such, we are willing to tolerate any type of behavior, but we have to love ourselves enough to be able to walk away from whatever is not edifying us.

Red Flags

No matter how in love you are, do not ignore the following red flags because they will give you a good indication of a person's true character:

- The person has no relationship with God.
- They have a habit of not keeping his or her word.
- They have a tendency of disrespecting his or her parents.
- The individual is rude to the servers at restaurants.
- They have a habit of not showing up on time for dates.

- The individual constantly talks about his or her former mate.
- Lacks good moral values.
- They have a tendency of criticizing and comparing you to others in negative ways.
- The person does not want his/her friends or relatives to know about you.
- They are always being negative in every aspect.
- They belittle you in front of others.
- The person disappears for days or weeks without contacting you.
- The individual seeks to change your moral values or may even criticize them.
- They get angry about small things.
- They are constantly praising him or herself.
- No set goals or dreams.
- The individual has a habit of being indecisive (changes his/her mind easily).
- The person keeps important secrets from you.
- They are constantly lying to you.
- They are unwilling to commit to the relationship.

God's Will

Here comes the moment in your life when you meet the person you have been praying for all along. You have a sense of peace that truly does surpass all understanding. When you reflect, you see the hand of God in it from the beginning. People who have chosen to wait *in* God and sought His voice, know the reward of experiencing God's perfect will for their lives.

> God's will doesn't bring confusion

They know God's will doesn't lack anything, and it brings joy and peace. So, why do so many believers reject God's perfect will and, instead, settle or create what they think is the perfect relationship?

When I started dating my husband, I knew he was the one for me when everything I have ever prayed for and asked God for was being answered one by one. God even gave me the smallest desires of my heart, which I didn't even realize I wanted but God knew that I needed and, to some degree, desired. He came at the perfect moment in my life, not when I was obsessively looking for him, but when I least expected it and with whom I least imagined.

Prior to marriage, my husband, Jesus, and I served a lot at church together, and we would have these deep, long conversations. One day while I was talking to him, I said to myself, "God, thank you for showing me that there are good guys out there, and respectful, loving and pure

It was a love that didn't change its mind

men do exist." Little did I know that the man with such great character who God was showing me was the man who He had picked out for me. Once I got the realization, I started to see life in a completely different way. Slowly, all the hurt and bitterness I had about men was being erased. Being with this man encouraged me to seek God more, and never in my life had I felt so sure about something.

Remember, God's will doesn't bring confusion, so if you feel the slightest doubt, then you know it's a sign for you to continue seeking the voice of God. Here are some reasons that we mistakenly stay in a relationship that we know is not the will of God:

- You have invested a lot of time or money
- Your families and/or friends are very close
- Everyone else thinks you are the "perfect couple"
- You planned the wedding or promised you would wed
- You have a strong physical attraction
- No one else is interested in you or shows you any kind of attention
- The other person is very attractive, wealthy and/or influential

Nothing you or anyone thinks, believes or feels should replace God's perfect will for your life. If God says no and shows you obvious signs, you should end the relationship no matter what. When you meet the one, God will show you, so trust Him by letting go of anything that doesn't align with the joy and peace that comes from experiencing His perfect will.

True Love

The longer I was with Jesus (my husband), the more that God used him to show me what real love is. It was a love that didn't change its mind and loved me even when I was acting a bit crazy. It was a love that was patient with me while God worked on my insecurities, and this love took care of me when I didn't know my way. He sought the Lord for our future and made sure that every decision we made was aligned to the will of God. Then, together, we got on this journey called marriage that has forever changed my life.

So, how do you know if a person is in the will of God for you? Who are you when you are with this person – stronger or weaker? Does this individual cause you to draw closer to God or do you feel this person is making you drift away? The answer is the word of God, which describes love, as God sees it.

The Bible says in 1 Corinthians 13:4-8:
> Love is patient, love is kind. It does not
> boast; it is not proud. It is not rude; it is
> not self-seeking; it's not easily angered; it

keeps no record of wrongs. Love does not delight in evil but rejoices with the truth. It always protects, always trust, always hopes, and always perseveres. Love never fails.

Love is patient: It's willing to wait to hear from God to make the next move. It doesn't rush things but desires to do things right. Love is patient with the other person. It waits for others and doesn't get angry if something is not completely to their satisfaction in the beginning.

Love is kind: It doesn't hurt the other person. It uses kind words when speaking. It doesn't disrespect the other person, but has a heart of compassion and kindness. It treats the person with the same caring shown to them by God.

Love does not boast; it is not proud: It doesn't think they are always right. It doesn't have a prideful attitude, but is willing to apologize and make things right as much as possible. It affirms the other person and seeks the best in their partner.

It is not self-seeking: It does not run the other way when they don't get what they want, and it is willing to lay down its own desires to please the other person.

It's not easily angered: It has so much love for the other person, so it's hard for them to get upset. They are willing to talk and communicate about anything, and they know that there is nothing that together they cannot solve.

It keeps no record of wrongs: Forgiveness is a way of life for them. You realize that the other person is human and that there will be times he/she makes mistakes, but you speak about what hurt you and you make the decision to completely forgive and never bring up what was done again. You forgive and you forget.

Love does not delight in evil but rejoices with the truth: You realize that together you are a team and can create a vision and goals that you both want to achieve. Life does not become a competition. You don't feel like you have to do something to impress the other person or to be better than the other person. You are so in love that when they are blessed, you are blessed, and when they are hurt, you are hurt.

Love always protects: You seek to protect them from harm. You don't speak badly about them and vice versa. You protect their imagine, and you are always looking out for their best interest.

Love always trust: You don't worry about them cheating on you or doing something bad because you have complete trust in who they are. They never give you a reason to doubt them. You trust them with your most inner thoughts and secrets.

Love always hopes: Based on God's plan and purpose, you create a mission statement together. You seek God together, and you realize that God has joined you together to complete one purpose and one assignment on Earth.

Love always preserves: You are always pushing to strengthen your relationship and to reach your goals together. If things are becoming a little bumpy, you don't give up, but you seek Godly advice. You persevere and push forward together.

Love never fails: Because what God has joined together, no man can ever separate.

God, when will I get married? I encourage you to look at that question in a different way now. God is preparing a way for you. He is setting up every single detail. Just like a GPS guides you and gives you directions, is the same way God is directing the answer to that prayer. Don't worry how you will get there or exactly when or what will happen. Just let God guide you on this journey, and be ready to make a left or right when He needs you to and He wants you to stop or yield. He will make sure you don't get lost.

Enjoy this road trip, every moment of it. While you are on your way, make sure you are the best person you can be because the exit to your question is coming up, and when you have reached the destination, you will begin one of the most amazing journeys of your life.

About the Author

At a very young age, I dreamed of writing books. As an introvert, my words were always best expressed in writing. Writing was used as my joy, as well as my escape. All I ever wanted is to minister to someone and touch their life with my words so that they are able to find hope and know that God is able to do the impossible and the unthinkable in their lives.

I was born and raised in Miami, Florida, with my younger and sister and brother. My mother went to be with the Lord when I was in my early twenties, and my Dad did everything he could to keep us together. My family is a huge part of what I write. Our journey and bond are examples of the wonderful love of God and how He gives us joy and peace that surpass all understanding.

I married my best friend and embarked on one of the most exciting journeys in my life, marriage. We spent many date nights dreaming and planning. Hours were spent over coffee, thinking of all the wonderful things that God has done and will be doing in our lives. With that, we decided to make a scary life-changing decision, leaving our jobs, packing our things, and moving to Lynchburg, Virginia so my husband can start Law School at Liberty University. In the midst of adapting to a new city, completing my Masters in Marriage and Family Counseling, working, missing or families, and enjoying our second honeymoon and freezing weather, my first book, *God, When Will I Get Married?* came together.

God, When Will I Get Married? is a very special book to me because it's a book I wish I had many years ago. If I could change someone's mentality or simply help someone know how much they are valued, then I know ever tear or heart break I experienced was completely worth it.

Contact the Author:

www.laurareyes.org

 GodWhenWillIGetMarried

 @laurareyes10

CPSIA information can be obtained
at www.ICGtesting.com
Printed in the USA
LVHW051939030520
654914LV00023B/2149